JOHN CORIGLIANO

CONCERTO FOR PIANO AND ORCHESTRA

ED 46676c

ISBN 0-634-00284-8

G. SCHIRMER, *Inc.*

PROGRAM NOTE

In this concerto the writing for both solo piano and orchestra is extremely virtuosic and theatrical. While the work is basically tonal, there are many atonal sections, and in the trio of the second movement there is a section of strict twelve-tone writing. The rhythms throughout the work are highly irregular and meters change often.

The first movement, the largest in scope, uses sonata-allegro form in an original way. After a few bars of introduction by the brass, the piano enters with a large cadenza accompanied by percussion and harp. This section introduces the first theme—a savage three-note motto (B-flat, B-natural, C). This highly energetic section reaches a peak climaxed by a piano run which concludes on the orchestra's opening note, E. A sudden *pianissimo* for the full orchestra signals a change of tempo and mood. The following lyrical orchestral *tutti* introduces and expands the movement's second theme—a *cantabile* melody first heard in the solo horn—and builds to a large orchestral climax. After this, the piano reenters, echoing its original three-note motto. A sudden change of tempo then introduces the development section, in which two opposed metamorphoses take place: each theme is developed separately. This separate development transforms the aggressive three-note motto into a lyrical theme, and the lyrical theme into a savage motto; in other words, each becomes the other. At the end of the development the first theme is heard in canon while the piano and brass toss about the second theme. The climax leads directly to a second cadenza which marks the beginning of the recapitulation, followed this time by a diabolic coda which brings the movement to an end.

The second movement is a short and fleet scherzo that breaks the emotional tension generated in the first movement. Three short repeated chords form the scherzo's motto, which is based on the superimposition of major and minor thirds. The trio is based on a twelve-tone row derived from the piano figures in the beginning of the movement.

In the third movement all the themes are based on six notes. The form is arch-shaped, building to a peak and diminishing to a hushed single-note piano melody which leads directly into the final movement: a rondo whose major theme, a *fugato*, utilizes orchestral and piano tone-clusters as an integral part of its structure. The three subsections of the movement incorporate the major themes from the earlier three movements, concluding with the original three-note motto of the first movement joining to end the concerto in a burst of virtuosic energy and color.

—John Corigliano

The Piano Concerto *was commissioned by the San Antonio Symphony.*

It was first performed April 7, 1968, at the opening concert of Hemisfair '68
in the new Theatre for the Performing Arts, San Antonio, Texas,
by Hilde Somer, soloist, with the San Antonio Symphony
conducted by Victor Alessandro.

INSTRUMENTATION

3 Flutes (1 doubling Piccolo)
3 Oboes (1 doubling English Horn)
3 Clarinets in B♭ (1 doubling Bass Clarinet)
2 Bassoons
Contrabassoon

4 Horns in F
3 Trumpets in C
3 Trombones
Tuba

Timpani
Percussion
Xylophone, Chime, Suspended Cymbal,
Tenor Drum, 3 Pitched Drums, Snare Drum,
Bass Drum, Tambourine, Whip, Ratchet

Harp

Solo Piano

Strings

duration: ca. 30 minutes

recordings on compact disc:

Barry Douglas, piano, with the St. Louis Symphony conducted by Leonard Slatkin
RCA Red Seal 09026-68100-2 *(1996)*

James Tocco, piano, with the Louisville Orchestra conducted by Lawrence Leighton Smith
Louisville Orchestra LCD 008 *(1994)*

Alain Lefèvre, piano, with the Pacific Symphony Orchestra conducted by Carl St. Clair
Koch International Classics 7250 *(1994)*

Performance material is available on rental.

for John Atkins

Concerto for Piano and Orchestra

John Corigliano

I

Copyright © 1971 by G. Schirmer, Inc. (ASCAP) New York, NY
International Copyright Secured. All Rights Reserved.
Warning: Unauthorized reproduction of this publication is prohibited by Federal law and subject to criminal prosecution.

46676c

ff
6
2
8
f secco
S.D.
T.D.
mp
p
(Xyl.)
f
(Timp.)

3

I

p secco

II

Cym.

p

(B. D.)

pp

p

p

(3 pitched drums)

4

p legg.

(Xyl.)

gliss.

p legg.

*) notes in ( ) may be omitted

15
8
I
II
sff p
cresc.
poco
a
poco
Cym.
pp
(chime)
6
ff
Cym.
S.D.
sfp

I
II
8
(Cym.)
L.H.
(med. Dr.)
p
gliss.
7
ff
sffz mf secco
sfz
(B. D.)
mp
cresc. e acc. poco
a
poco

I
A Tempo
8
ten.
(A Tempo)
fff
(ten.)
fff
ten.
8
A Tempo
mp
sf
ten.
(A Tempo)
II
Tamb.
Timp.
Cym.
sfp
sfz
cresc.
as fast as possible
slapstick
sffz
cresc.

*) Piano I can take top staff to 12 to facilate rehearsal.

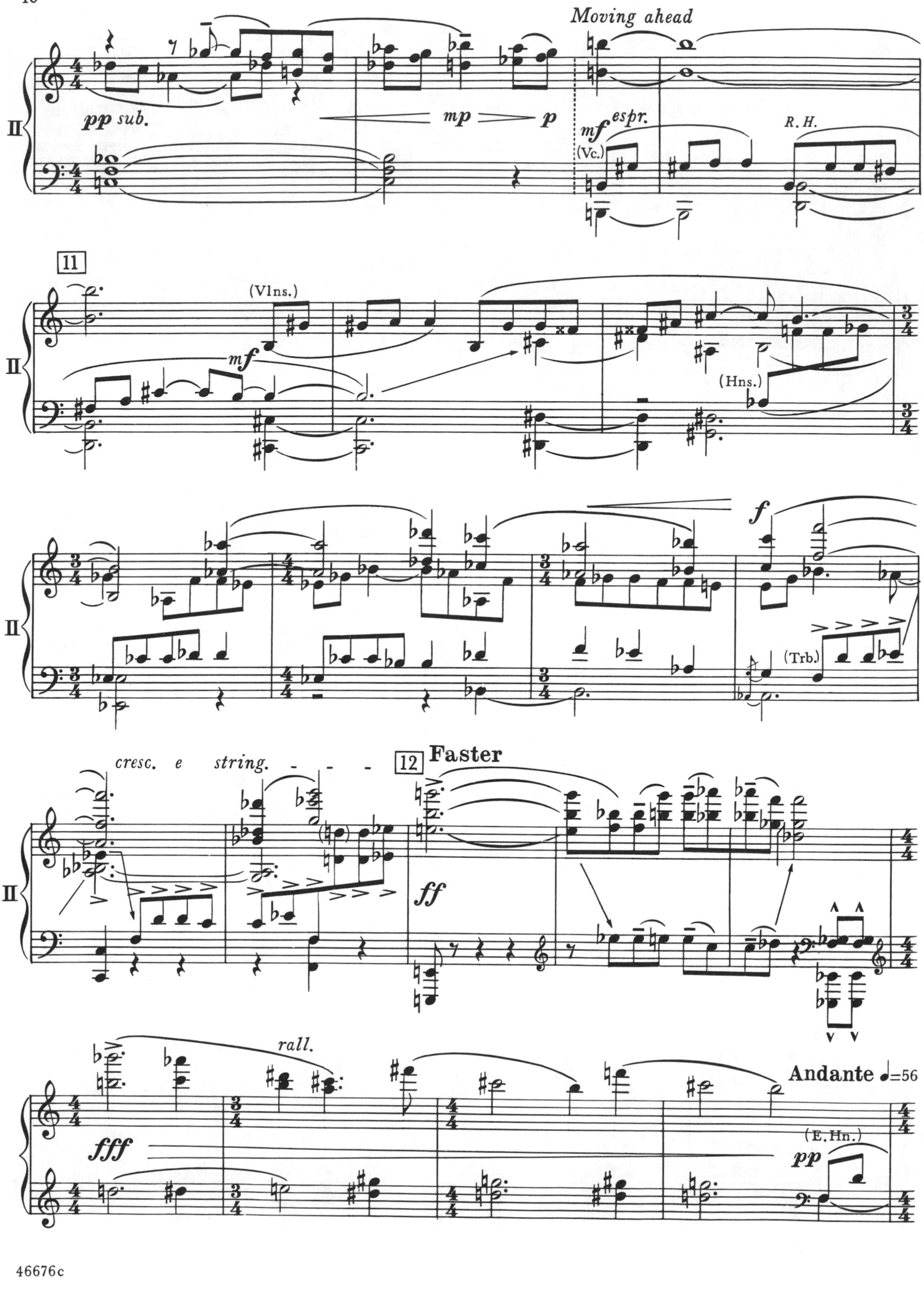

Moving ahead

II

pp sub. *mp* *p*

mf espr.

(Vc.)

R. H.

11

(Vlns.)

mf

(Hns.)

f

(Trb.)

cresc. e string.

12 **Faster**

ff

13
(Depress without sounding)
ppp legatissimo
I
II
(Cl.)
rall.
Allegro (Tempo I°)
(p)
sfp
p
(Fl.)
rall.
14
(pizz.)
(wws)

B. D.
p
(R.H.)
(Stgs.)
(L.H.)
15
mf
pp
5
15
gliss.
(Bns.)
mp

I
sempre p
II
(Stgs.)
(Ob.)
cresc.
poco
mp
8
16
cresc.
f
16
a
poco
(Tutti)
f

I
II
dim.
dim.
poco
a
poco
p legg.
pp
(wws)
p secco
17
f
(Stgs.)
17
f

(♪= ♪)
I
II
ff
8
18
(Tutti)
sfz
(Hns.)

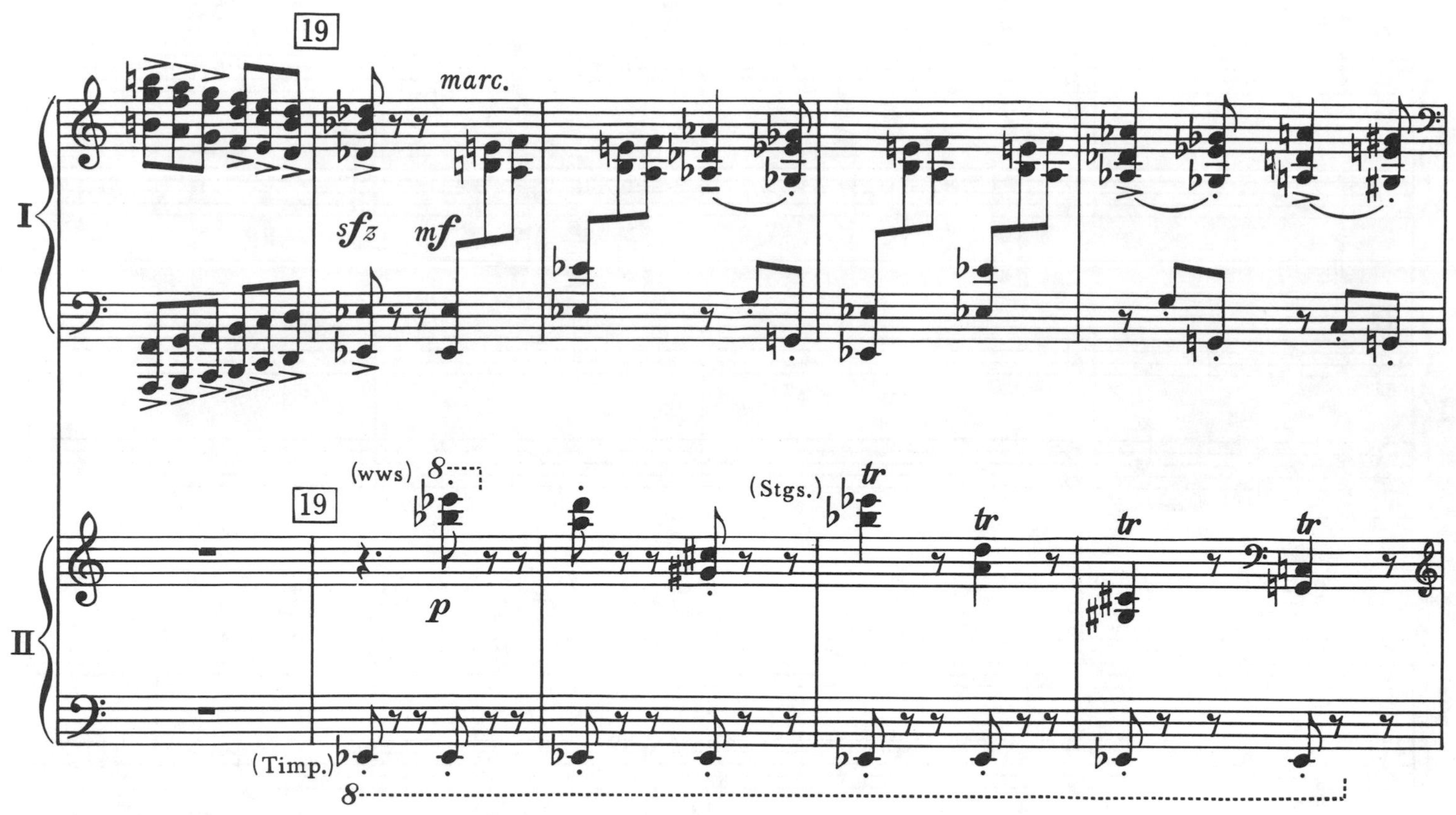
19
marc.
sfz
mf
I
(wws)
8
(Stgs.)
tr
19
p
II
(Timp.)
8

4
sfz
I
9
8
6
8
(Hn.)
II

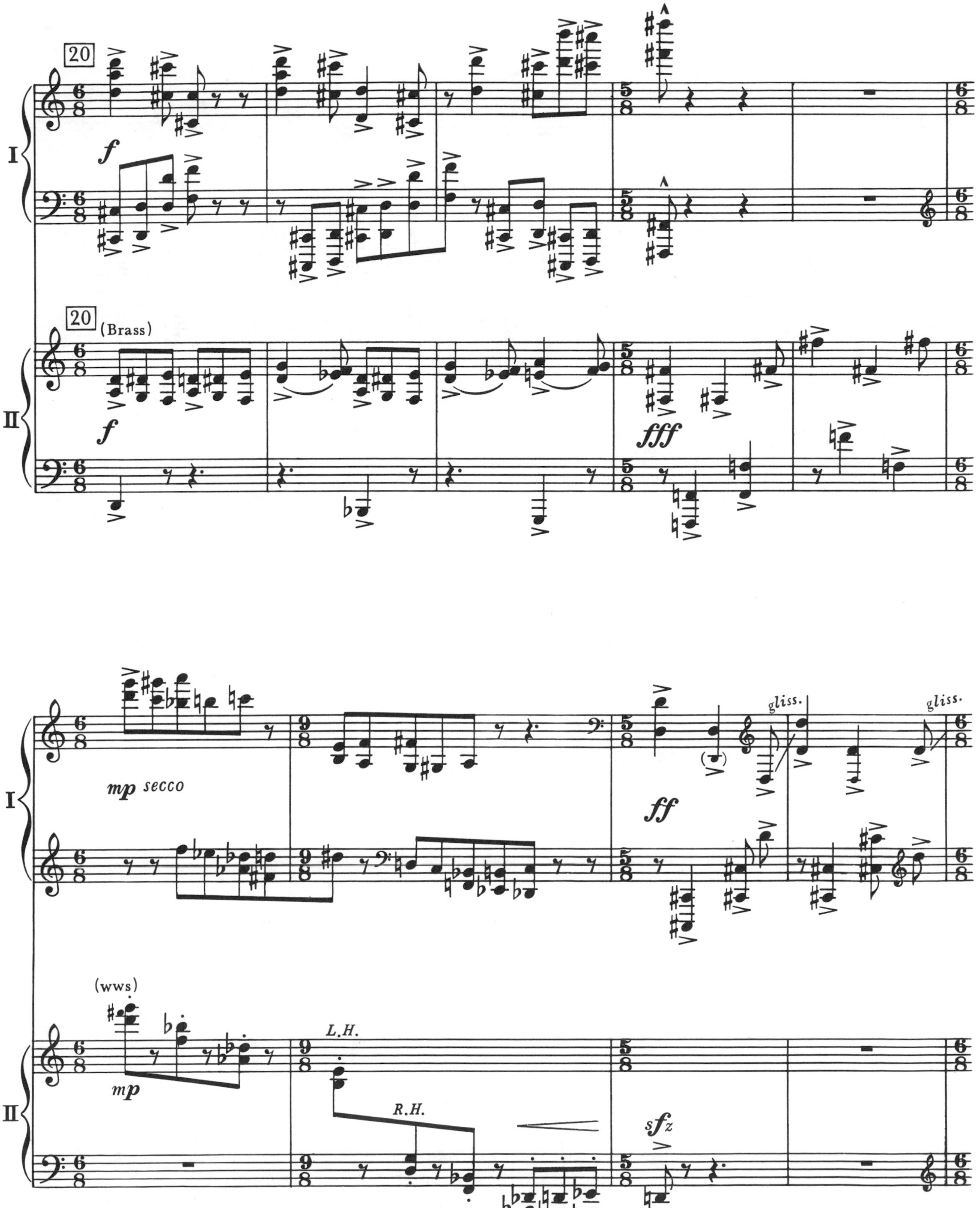

I
mp secco
ff
gliss.
gliss.

(wws)
II
mp
L.H.
R.H.
sfz

21
I
pp
21
(Stgs. pont.)
sfp
II
21
II
sfp
I
mp secco
II
pp
pp
pp
pp
(pizz.)
II

22
I
mp
cresc.
22
II
(Stgs.)
mp
(♭)
cresc.
poco
a
poco
(f)
(Brass)
mf
mf
sempre cresc.
(Tutti)
f
f

23
I
ff
23
II
f
(sempre a tempo)
tutta forza
sffz
(sempre a tempo)
(Stgs.)
fff
mf legato
sffz
II

poco rall.
I
poco rall.
(wws)
mp
p
II
Poco meno mosso
p (simply)
I
Poco meno mosso
(Hn.)
p
II
(pizz.)
p
pp
I
(Stgs.)
p
II

25
R.H.
p
25
cresc.
(Stgs.)
f
dolce
f
mp
mp
f
dim.
mf
dim.
p
(Hns.)
p
p

Rit.
p
I
II
(Stgs.) p
Meno mosso
27
rall.
depress. silently with S.P.
(Cls.)
Andante
ppp (legato)
ppp
(Stgs.)

28
Moving Ahead
I
Moving Ahead
28
(w.ws)
pp
(Hns.)
(Stgs.)
II
Faster ♩=92-100
p legato
6
Faster ♩=92-100
p
(Stgs.)
29
29
(+ Trb.)

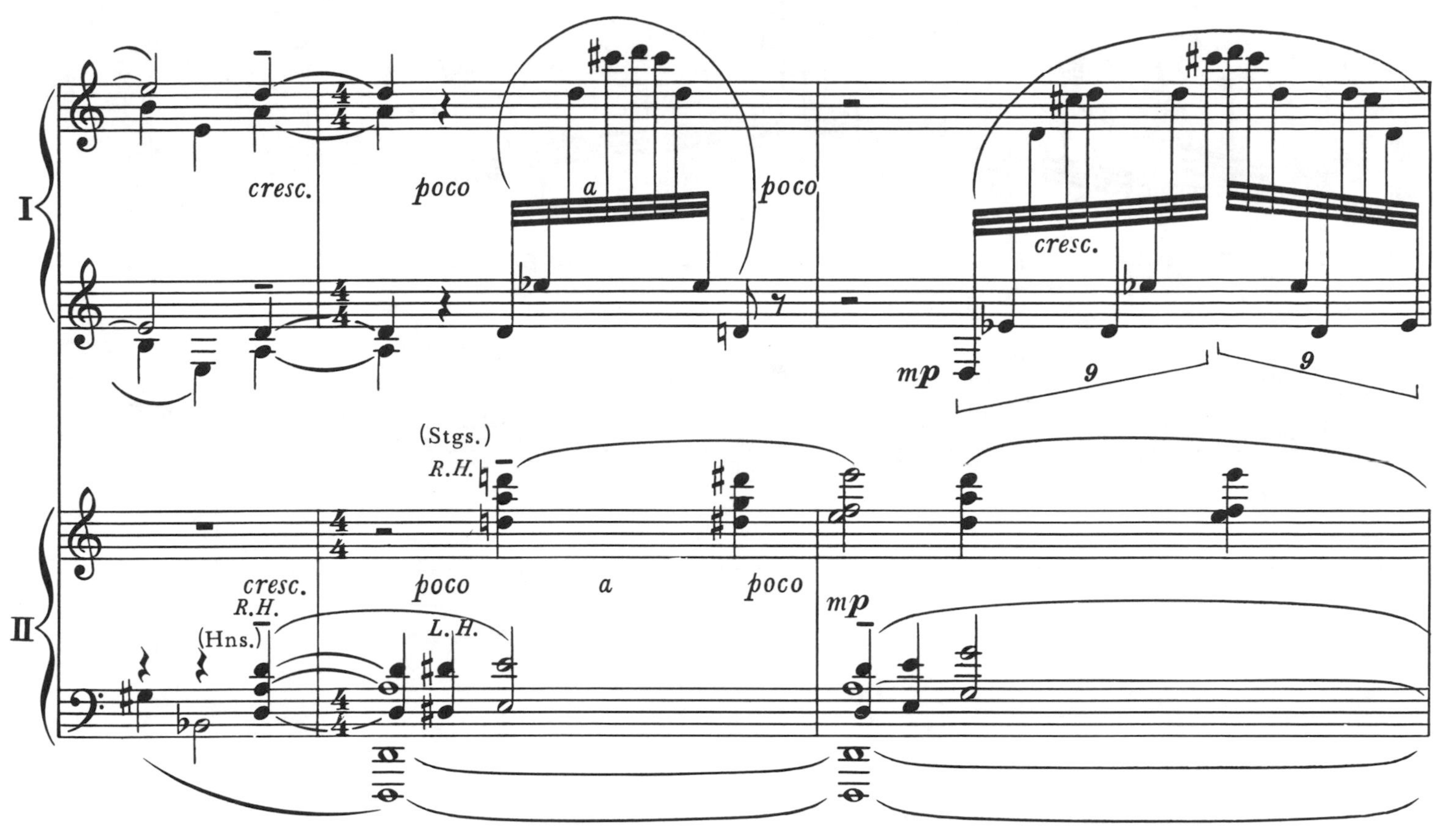

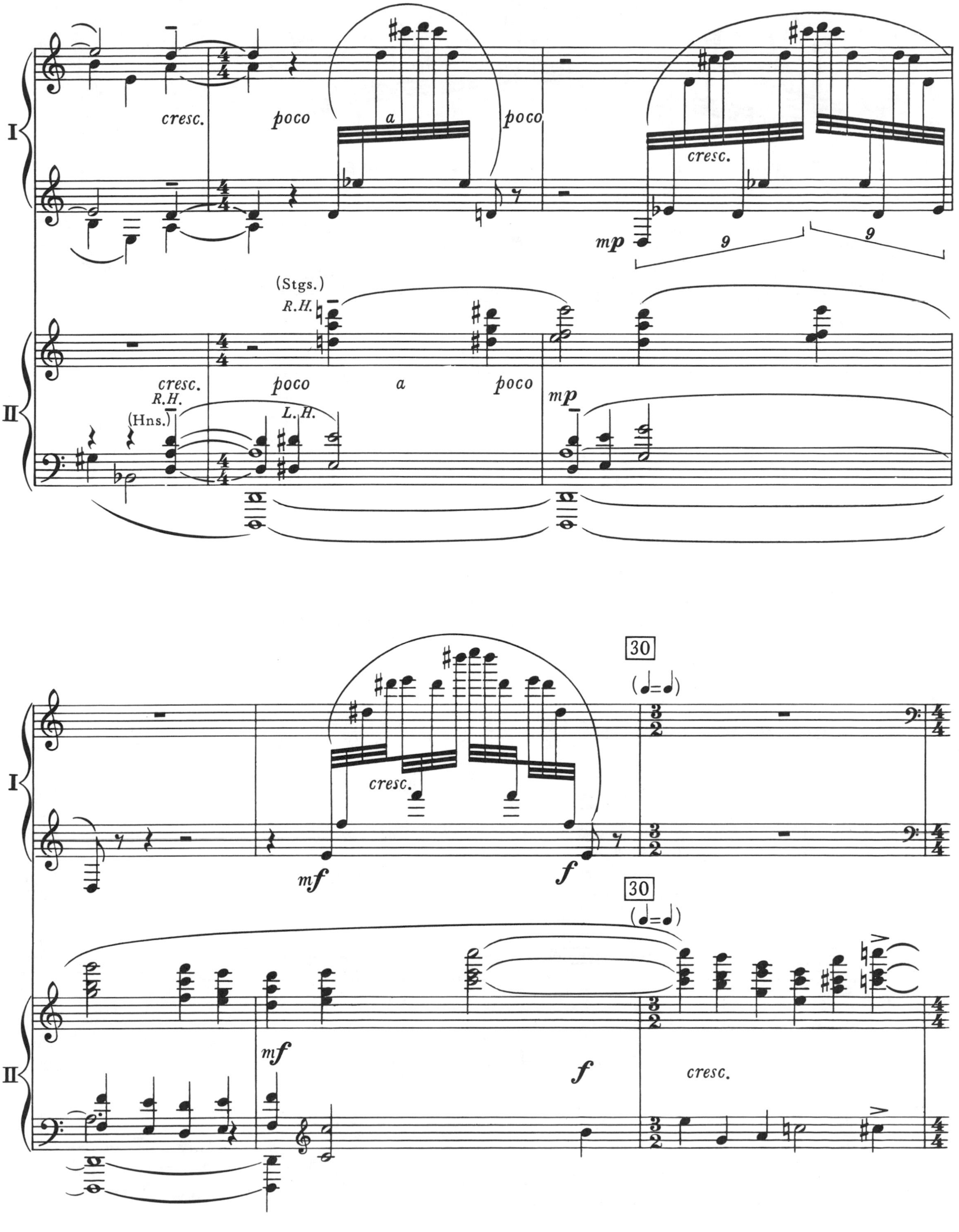

30

(♩=♩)

I

cresc.

mf

f

30

(♩=♩)

II

mf

f

cresc.

accel.

(quasi Cadenza)

I

ff

5

accel.

II

8

R.H.

I

fff

L.H.

R.H.

R.H.

L.H.

sfz

Allegro ♩=120
31
I
II
(Tutti)
ff
fff
possible
sffz
tr♮
tr
tr♭

32
Presto 𝅗𝅥. = 84–92
I
II
sff
sfffz
f
(Stgs.)
R. H.
L. H.
sfz
mf
gliss.
simile
(Hns.)
mp
sfp
(Tutti)

33
I
ff
33
R.H.
(wws)
L.H.
II
sfz
mp
7
gliss.
(Vlns)
R.H.
L.H.
34
34
ff
sfz

35
35
I
II
ff marc.
sfz
sfz
ff
(Stgs.+ Brass)
ff
f
36
mf marc.
(wws)
36
(Stgs.)
mp sempre legato

I
II
6
mp
(Trb.)
mf
mp
5
37
f
37
(Hns.)
L.H.
mf

I
II
(Hns.)
R.H.
f
glis.
ff
secco
38
38
mp
(Brass)

I
gradual dim.
gliss.
(f)
II
gradual cresc.
cresc.
mp
p
(niente)
L.H.
f
ff
fff
poss.

Molto Allegro (Tempo I°)
39
14
fff
L.H.
39
Molto Allegro (Tempo I°)
B. D.
sffffz
8
14
L.H.
R.H.
R.H.
L.H.
R.H.
10:6
L.H.
(Xyl.)
f
S.D.
T.D.

7:4
I
40
7
6
10
fff
mp
p
(Xyl.)
8
3
f
(Susp. Cym.)
II
B.D.
I
II

*) notes in ( ) may be omitted

42
I
II
fff
(Timp.)
ff
43

15
8
8
I
sf p
cresc.
poco
II
(chime)
8
a
poco
Susp. Cym.
p
cresc.
ff
L.H.
(Tutti perc.)
sffz secco

I
II
sffz
simile
simile
sffz

I
II
(Cymb.)
fff secco
dim.
poco
a
poco
sffz
sffz
poco rall.
dim.
44
Andante ♩=56
pp
Andante ♩=56
(Vlns.) 8
44
poco rall.
pp

8
(Ob.)
(Fl.)
pp
II
(Cl.)
pp
I
mp (simply)
pp
8
(Stgs.)
45
Moving Ahead
p legato
3
8
(Cl.)

S. P.

I
II
I
II
mp (Stgs.)
46
I
II
46
mf

I
II
Poco meno mosso
47
(Fl.)
(Stgs.)
rall.
(Cl.)

48
Allegro (Tempo I°)
I
p secco
5
48
Allegro (Tempo I°)
II
p secco
B. D.
(w.ws)
(3 dr.)
(pizz.)
(w.ws)
R. H.
L. H.
pp
49
sempre p
(Cl.)
49
mp
(Tpt.)
(Stgs.)

I
II
mp
Glock.
(w.ws)
R.H.
L.H.
50
f
(Tpt.)
p secco

51
I
(Stgs.)
f
51
II
ff
sffz
(Tutti)
ff
8
ff
gliss.
(w.w.s)
ff

52
I
f secco
52
II
f (Tutti)
L.H.
R.H.
L.H.
f
f
53
(Brass)
fff
(+ Str.)

Poco Rit. (optional)
54
ff
I
Poco Rit. (optional)
54
II
Broadly
10
10
10
12
fff
I
Broadly
(Tutti)
II
black keys
white keys
fff
blk
whte
(Xyl.)
5
fff
Cym.
ff
fff
Tam Tam
fff

55
Molto Allegro
sffz
I
(Tutti)
55
sffz
Molto Allegro
cresc.
poco
II
(Xyl.)
sff
mp
Cym.
S. D.
pp
cresc.
mp
(Brasses)

I

II

mp 6 *cresc.* *poco* *a* *poco*

a *poco*

ff 7 8 *loco* 5 *fff* *sfffz* *sfffz*

S. D.

B. D.

8 *fff* *fff* *sffz* 8 8

II

♩.= 108 (♩= 144)
Scherzo
(♪=♪)
I
p e legg.
II
mp (w.w.s, Hp.)
10
(Brass)
sfz
gliss.
mf
sfz
mp
mf

simile
I
f
II
mf
sfz
(Str.)
p
loco
p
p secco
8
p
(Bns.)
1
sffz (f)
(p)
(f)
sffz
cresc.
poco
a
poco

(loco)
sffz
sffz
sffz
mp
cresc.
8
I
simile
f
ff
2
sfffz
p
pp
II
(Timp.)
(Str.)
(Ob.)

I
II
(Bn.)
pp
p (wws)
(♪=♪)
3
p
(p) (+ Stgs., pizz.)
mf
f
(Solo Vn., Fl.)
gl.
gliss.
mp
(wws)

I
ff sub.
II
(Xyl.)
sfz
sfz
sfz
sfz
sfz
(Stgs.)
sff
(ff)
8
loco
fff
(Tutti)
ff
fff

4 Misterioso
pp legato
I
ffff
(Hp.)
mf
molto
p
II
4 Misterioso
pp
legato
(Fl.)
legato
(Bn.)
secco
p
(Stgs.)
p secco
R.H.
L.H.
L.H.

I
II
5
loco
8
gl.
f
ff
sffz
f (Tutti)

I
II
(Stgs.)
6
6
(wws)
(Trb.)
(pizz.)

7 Tempo I°
I
fff
7 Tempo I°
II
ff (Tutti)
ff
ff
8
sffz
(Stgs.)
fffff
molto secco
molto dim.
8
(Timp.)
p
8 f
mf
mp
(B. D.) 8

I
II
S.D.
p
8
sf
mp secco
(Brass; Timp.)
f
sffz
sub. p
sfp
(Tutti)
p secco
p
loco
cresc.
poco
f
sffz
cresc.
poco

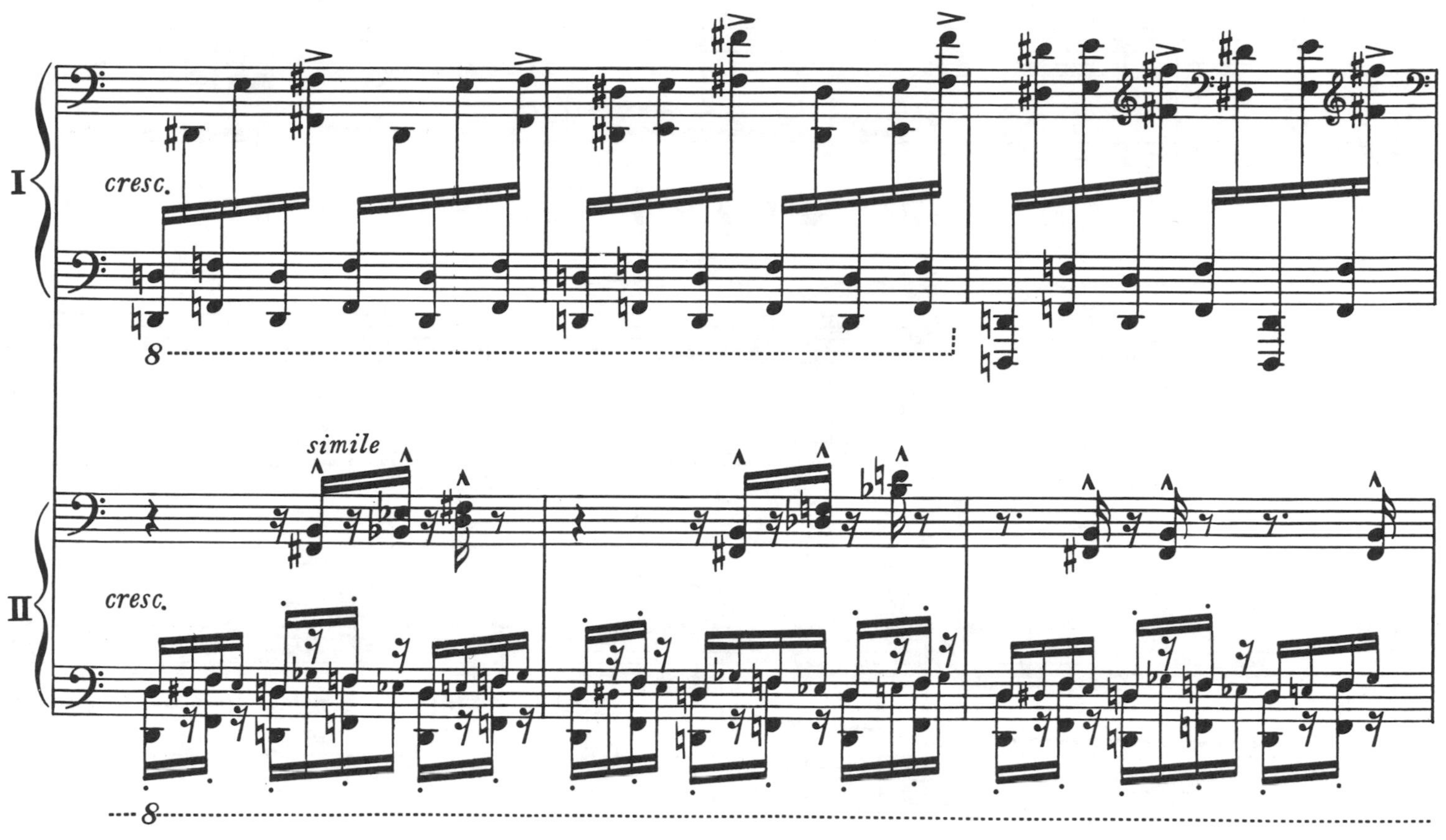

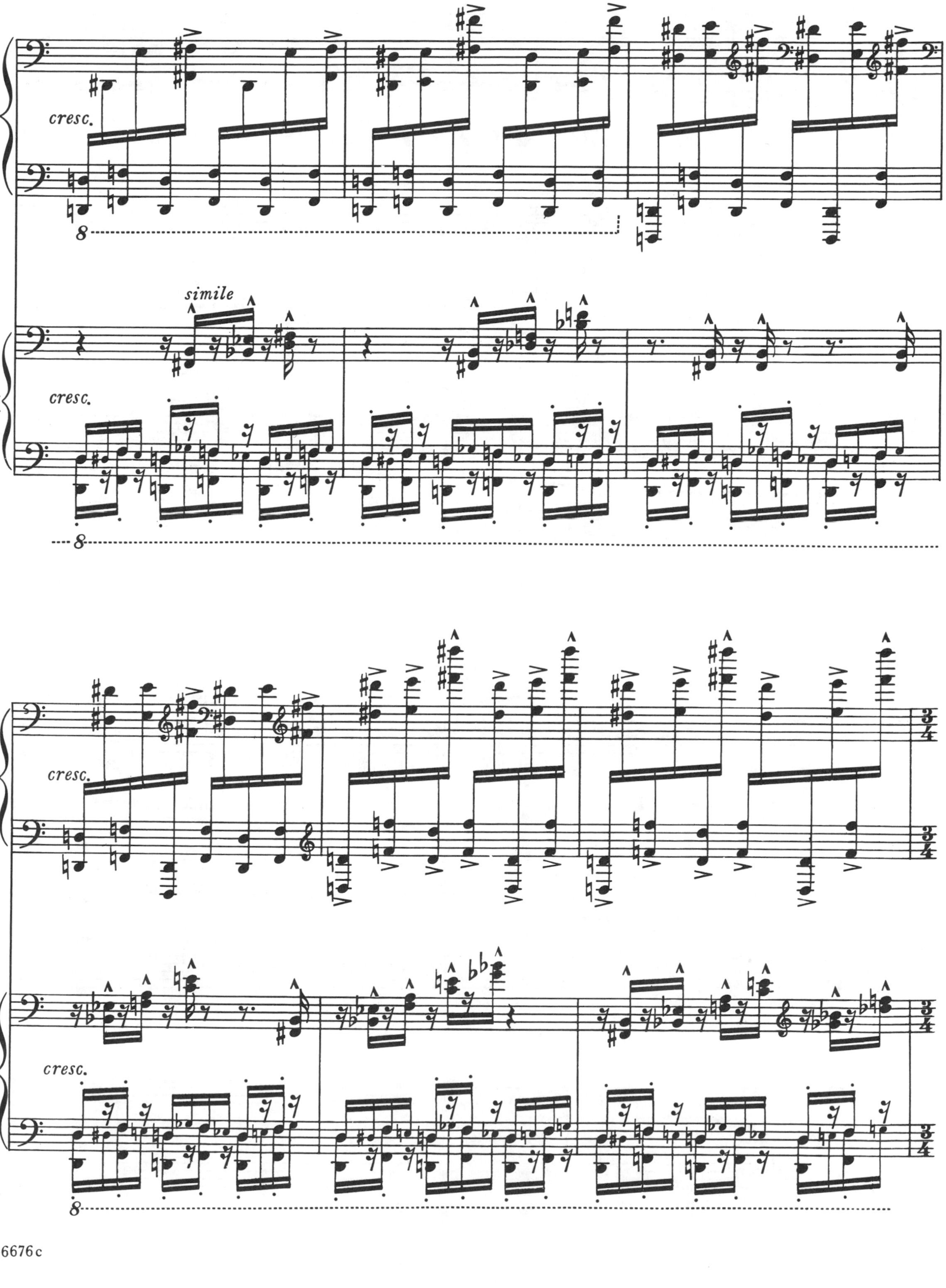
I
cresc.
8
simile
II
cresc.
8
I
cresc.
II
cresc.
8

9
I
II
molto
(Timp.)
(Stgs.)
(Ob.)
(+ Bn.)
(Brass)

8
10
I
8
mf
f
(Fl.)
II
(wws)
p
mp
mf
ff sub.
(Tpts.)
f

8
I
II
11
11
sfffz
(wws)
mp
(Brass)
sffz
ff marc.
f
p secco
(Stgs.)
p
dim.
f
mf
mp
secco
mf
mp

simile
I
II
dim.
pp
(p)
(w.w.s)
pp
gliss.
(Stgs.)
pp
ppp
pp
ppp
8
(w.w.s)
8
pp
ppp

III

Appassionato ♩=72
II
ff
(Stgs.)
sfz
sfz
sfz
sfz
1
Faster ♩=88
I
1
Faster ♩=88
ff
(Brass)
dolce
II
ff
mf
f
I
rall.
mf
mp
(Bn.)
dim.
rall.
p

2
Tempo Iº
I
pp legatissimo
2
Tempo Iº
II
(B.Cl.)
(Bn.)
3
3
(Fls.)
legatissimo
(Stgs.)
3

I
II
p
4
Moving a bit faster
4
Moving a bit faster
mp (Stgs.)
3
mp
3
(Fl.)

I
II
(Hns.)
mf
5
I
II
5
mf
f
f (dolce)
I
II
(Tutti)
f espr.

I
II
f
sub.
mp
cresc.
6
loco
sffz
8
R.H.
L.H.

I

II

sffz secco

sffz

ff

ff

sffz

sffz

sf

mp

secco

mp

8

Stringendo poco

I

II

ff

a
poco
I
f
a
poco
II
7
A Tempo
I
fff
7
A Tempo
II
sffz
(Susp. Cym.)
mp
8
I
8
II
ff

stringendo poco a poco
cresc. poss.
II
S.D.
mf
(wildly)
3
ffff (poss.)
I
6
5
8
sfffz
(Tenor Dr.)
ff
cresc.
S.D.
sfz
sffz
p
Fls; (Stgs.)
9
Slower
(Ob.)
(Bn.)
(Fl.)
(Cl.)
ten.
acc.
legatissimo

I

II

(2 Cls.)

a tempo

pp legatissimo

pp

I

II

8

I

II

10

8

10 (Ob.)

pp

(L.H.)
rall.
a tempo
ppp
(Stgs.)
(wws)
(Hn.)
11
cresc.
dim.
mp
mf
a tempo
(Ob.)
pp

I
II
(Serenely)
(Stgs.)
(Hn.)
(Cl.)
p
pp
(pizz.)
(wws)
(Ob.)
(Stgs.)
Attacca Allegro
Attacca Allegro

IV

2
3
I
tr
f marc.
(Fl.)
B.D.
ratchet
sfz
II
(wws)
(+ Stgs. pizz.)
mf
(R.H.)
4
* ♮♯♭ custer at base of keyboard

5
I
II
(Hrp.)
gliss.
mp secco
(Xyl; hrp.)
sfz
(Stg. cluster)
6
(Tpts. wws)
mp
sfz

I
II
sfz
mf secco
(Stgs.)
mf
7
p
(Brass cluster)

8
I
II
(Fl; Bn.)
p
mp
8
9
sfz
mf
mf marc.
(Trb.)
9

Ossia
I
II
(Fl.)
mp
mf
f
10
(Tpt; Xyl.)
sfz
(Trbs.)

I
II
sf
ff
(Tpts.)
f
(Hns.)
cresc.
sfz
sf
11
sfz
(Tutti)
S.D.
(Trbs.)
f

12
I
II
ff
8
ff
I
II
mf
13
I
II
(Timp.)
f

14
I
II
S.D.
f
(Trb.)
6
5
8
(wws, hrp)
15
mf cresc.
sf
sfz
(Trbs)
mf

I
II
(Hns)
(Tpts)
(Tutti)
sfz
8
ff

17
I
gliss.
ff
II
(Tpts)
gliss.
(Tutti)
cresc.
(3 Dr.)
B.D.
(Ratchet)

Slightly slower

poco stringendo

18

I

fff sfff poss. sffz sffz sffz sffz

8

Slightly slower

18

* Palm clusters *(white keys)* *f poss. secco*

II

sffz

19

a tempo

8

I

sffz sffz sfffz (ffff) sffz dim. - poco - -

* Palm clusters - *R.H. Chromatic clusters*
L.H. white key clusters

a tempo

19

II

ffff (Tutti) dim. poco a poco fff

I
II
ff
a
poco
f
dim. mf
mp
p
(Bn.)
20
(♩.=138)
(Stgs)
(Hns.)
secco
(wws)
sfz
21
p legato

I
II
legato as possible
8
secco
simile
22
sfz
(Tpts)
f
sim.
L.H.
legato
molto

I
II
(wws)
mp secco
ff
(Hns.)
f
8
23
(Hn.)
gliss.
(Trb.)
(Timp.)
(pizz.)
decresc.
p

 *) grace note figures played on the beat.

* optional 6 Bar Violin solo doubles piano melody.

I
II
27
sfz
mf
f
(Hns.)
27

Ossia
I
II
(Fl; Tpt., Xyl.)
Ossia
I
II

*) Mark top voice

29
I
secco
mf
29
II
(♪=♪)
f
cresc.
L. H. Ossia
(Str.)
(Brass)

*) Mark top voice

31
I
f
ff
II
L.H.
ff (Hns.)
R.H.
fff
sffz
L.H.
sim.
ff
cresc.
(Brass)
fff
sim.
32

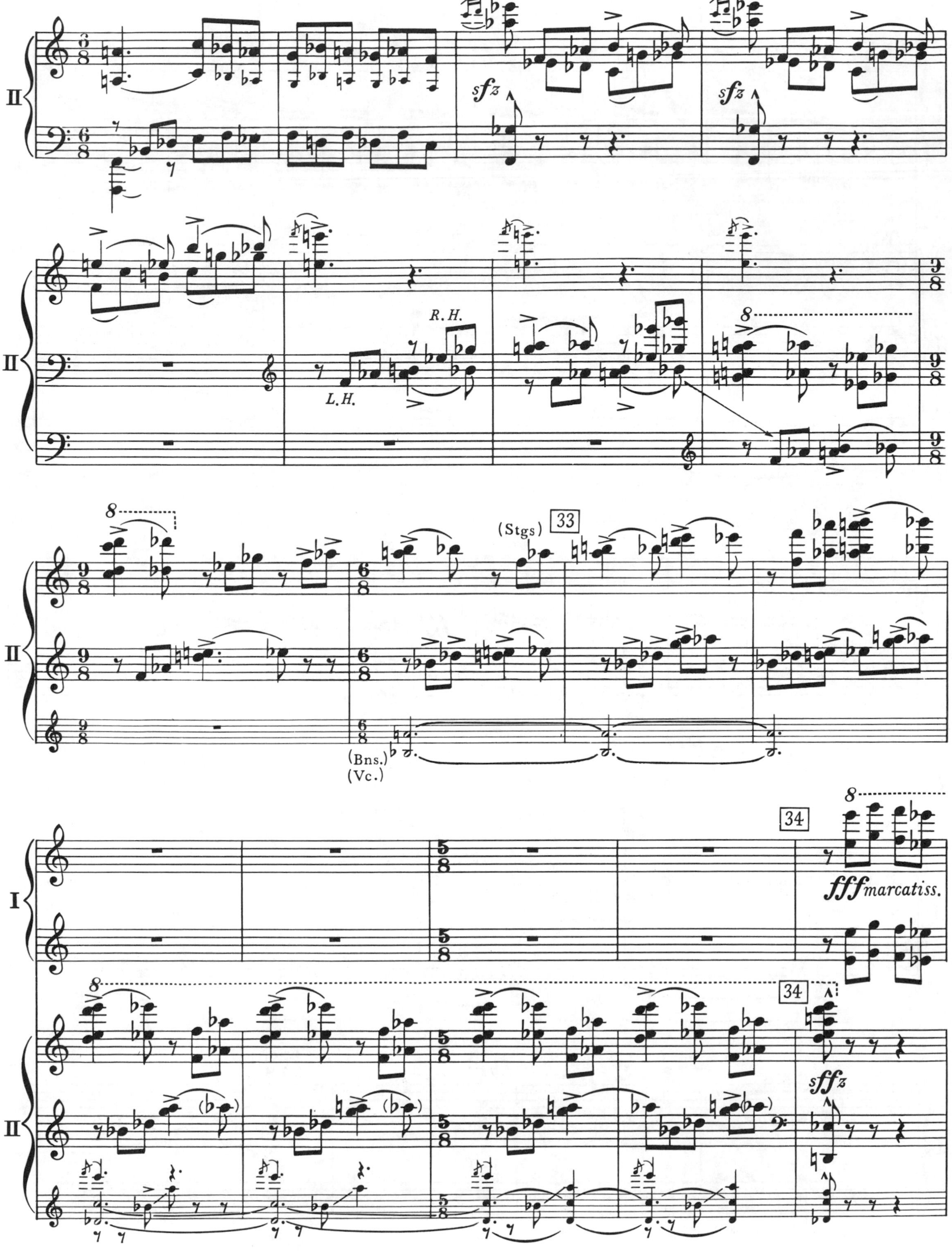

II
sfz
sfz
R.H.
L.H.
II
8
(Stgs)
33
II
(Bns.)
(Vc.)
34
I
fff marcatiss.
8
34
II
sffz

* Palm clusters *(white keys)*

** Palm clusters - *R.H. white key clusters*
L.H. chromatic clusters

I
II
sffz
sffz
ff
(Brass)
L.H.
mf
(Stgs. wws.)

36
8
loco
I
ff
36
sff
II
sffz
(Trbs.)
sffz
I
(Hns.)
(Tpts.)
II
(Tutti)

37
cresc.
8
gliss.
fff
I
37
cresc.
ff
II
R.H.
L.H.
(wildly)
(loco)

*) Palm clusters *(white keys)*
**) Palm clusters *(chromatic)*

mf
marc.
I
II
mp
(Timp.)
cresc.
poss.
8
sffz
poss.
f
cresc.
5